SOUTH EA
RAILWAY JOURNEYS

Through Malaysia

Written by
Mike Sharrocks

Graphics and layout design by Cheryl Reyes

Photographs taken by Mike Sharrocks

December 2015

August 2016 (Revised Edition)

www.mikesharrocks.com

Contents

Preface

Global tourism has grown dramatically during the last twenty years. With this growth has come a greater fracturing of the tourism market and the development of specialised interests or niche markets. Increasingly, travelers are becoming more discerning and demanding about what they expect to get from their holidays. More people who travel want to experience a genuine insight into foreign cultures or to see how people live their lives. There is also a greater desire to see environmental and social responsibility needs being met in the places that tourists stay in or visit. Added to this is the notion of 'slow tourism' where, instead of rushing from one place to another as fast as possible, people want to travel in a leisurely manner and take their time, perhaps as an antidote to hectic working lives.

Tenom-Halogilat Carriage

This is where rail travel has the potential to fit in. Traveling by train has moved on from the sole preserve of railway enthusiasts and emerged into an insightful means of visiting a country. This can be central to the enjoyment and purpose of the journey and can offer a rare perspective of an area, either through the people one meets on the train or indeed through the landscapes that one sees. Railway travel more often than not avoids the tourist traps and package tour crowds. The train systems can also reflect the particular culture or character of the country. One can cover significant distances and, at the same time, relax, read, or just gaze out of the window.

Tenom to Halogilat Scenery, Sabah

This travelogue describes the seventh of a series of long distance journeys through South East Asia. It deals with train travel through Malaysia and specifically with two routes: the North Borneo Railway from Tanjung Aru (Kota Kinabalu) to Tenom; and, along the western part of Peninsular Malaysia from Singapore (Woodlands) to Alor Star (and on to Langkawi Island). A third main railway route ('The Jungle Line') from Gemas to Tumpat on the northeastern coast of Peninsular Malaysia could also be a future possibility, although this line is currently out of operation. The purpose of the travelogue is to explore railway travel as a more leisurely means of tourism. There are some basic principles, or *modus operandi*, for travel, as follows:

- Scheduled railway services were chosen for all journeys and not bespoke luxury train services;

Hokkien Temple Door, Melaka

- Journeys were booked on an ad hoc basis with little advance notice (except perhaps obtaining a ticket a day or two ahead);
- Travel would, as far as possible, be undertaken during the day so that both urban and rural landscapes could be seen;
- Where possible, the most comfortable travel class was chosen. This would fit in with the notion of 'leisurely' travel as opposed to seeking the cheapest option. Similarly, recommended accommodation is based not on a cost-saving basis but on character and comfort; and,
- Overnight stops were determined by the distance traveled during the day, rail schedules and by their tourism attractiveness.

The travelogue style is intended to be anecdotal and illustrative (with photos) and to give the reader an idea of the sort of experiences (good and bad) that could be expected in undertaking the trip. Although some factual information is provided for the routes traveled, this does not include railway schedules (which are continuously changing anyway). There is no attempt to be a comprehensive tourist guide and the information provided is indicative. Other dedicated travel guides would be able to offer a more complete coverage of attractions and accommodation.

North Borneo Railway

North Borneo Railway: Kota Kinabalu to Tenom

"Sometimes the wrong train will take you to the right station"
– Shaikh to Fernandes in the Indian film 'The Lunchbox'

Sabah State Railway (SSR) operates the only railway route in Malaysian Borneo from Tanjung Aru Station (Kota Kinabalu) to Beaufort and Tenom, a distance of 134kms (see route map). This route was formerly known as the North Borneo Railway Line. There has been a five-year upgrade of the railway system prior to its reopening in February 2011.

A reinstatement of the short section from Tanjung Aru to the centre of Kota Kinabalu

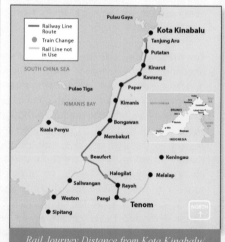

Rail Journey Distance from Kota Kinabalu/ Tanjung Aru to Tenom (134 kms/83 miles)

is under consideration. There is also a heritage rail component operated jointly by Sutera Harbour Resort and SSR that runs from Tanjung Aru to Papar.

Keretapi Tanah Melayu (KTM), the national railway operator for Peninsular Malaysia, has been working with SSR to improve safety along the route. SSR is part of the Sabah State administration. The section from Beaufort to Tenom is particularly prone to disruption due to landslips and engine problems. There have been two recent accidents: one in 2011 when a train from Tanjung Aru to Beaufort collided with a fuel tanker at a railway crossing, where there were injuries but no fatalities; and, in April 2008, when a train plunged into the River Padas gorge near Tenom killing two people.

The SSR website (www.railway.sabah.gov.my) is available in English and includes train schedules. Tickets can only be bought on the day of travel at railway stations (where English is spoken). It's advisable to ring the station to check up on service and operational issues: Tanjung Aru station (+60-(0)88262536); Beaufort station (+60-(0)87211518); and, Tenom station (+60-(0)87735514).

DAY 1
Kota Kinabalu

Initial impressions of Kota Kinabalu were of its ramshackle appearance. It was rebuilt after extensive destruction during WWII when the town, then known as Jesselton, was occupied by the Japanese. Nowadays, there seems to have been a popular adoption of blue corrugated cladding and roof tiling, especially for public buildings, perhaps to blend in with blue skies. A second popular choice appears to be green roofing and cladding with its apparent potential to merge with a background of lush greenery. These roofscape themes disappear in the central gridiron part of Kota Kinabalu where 1950s to 1970s concrete construction predominates with poorly maintained high-rise buildings. At least the centre has some urban cohesion in contrast to thrown-together buildings on the outskirts where energetic building construction is evident. New shopping malls and apartment blocks have been popping up with names like 'The Loft' and 'KK Times Square'. Traffic congestion is beginning to be a problem.

In general, there is a half forgotten quality to Kota Kinabalu with the city struggling to establish its visual identity. The centre is roughly oblong in shape and hemmed in between the South China Sea waterfront and steeply rising slopes covered in forest and dense vegetation. Perhaps the most characterful part was Jalan Gaya, formerly known as Bond Street during the British colonial time, with a Chinatown-style arch entrance. Some of the street has been pedestrianised with tall trees providing shading. There are shop houses and traditional cafes (*kedai kopi*), restaurants and bakeries. Parts of the city centre also have a backpacker feel, especially around Australia Place between Jalan Gaya and the Signal Hill slopes, which was where Australian troops were billeted soon after the end of WWII.

Australia Place Flat Iron Building

North Borneo Railway

Jalan Gaya Shop, Chinatown

Visitors to Kota Kinabalu generally use the city as a base for trips to wildlife areas and indigenous tribal villages, such as for the Mari Mari and Kadazan-Dusun. There are a number of national parks in the area including the most famous, Kinabalu National Park with trekking routes to the top of Mount Kinabalu, as well as the national parks of Crocker Range and Pulau Tiga, amongst others. Many tourists also make a stop in Kota Kinabalu to go further afield to Sabah's east coast and the Semporna Archipelago, especially for diving in Sipadan. In 2000 the Sipadan area created headline news when the Islamic group, Abu Sayyaf, kidnapped 21 tourists and resort workers and took them to the Philippines. Abu Sayyaf attacked resorts and fishing villages again during 2013-2014 when there were also incursions by Filipino groups in support of the Sultanate of Sulu's claims to parts of the east coast of Sabah.

I stayed in the Jesselton Hotel at the northern end of Jalan Gaya, built by Hong Kong contractors as the first post-war hotel in 1954 during the city's reconstruction. Subsequently, the property was completely renovated in the 1980's. A London taxi is available for guests. A doorman in white pith helmet, white shirt and shorts greets visitors, of which the most famous included Lady Mountbatten and Mohammad Ali (in 1975).

Signal Hill Trail

In the morning I left the hotel to climb up the steep slopes of Signal Hill and the city centre's forested backdrop. I was warned to be careful as there had been muggings along the footpaths there. It was hot and sunny and I climbed the short boardwalk section of the Signal Hill Jungle Trail up to Jalan Bukit Bendera, which follows the forested escarpment parallel to the length of Kota Kinabalu city centre. At the end of the trail, unharmed, I walked the short distance along the road to the Signal Hill

Observatory, a café with panoramic views over the city centre, coastline and port. The South China Sea glistened in the distance.

City Centre View

From the Observatory I went southwards along Jalan Bukit Bendera through the forest to the Atkinson Clock Tower. This is a distinctive white wooden landmark built in 1905 to honour the town's first district officer who died of malaria in his twenties. I continued along Jalan Istana towards the palace (*istana*) where large houses and government buildings were set amongst the dense forest. There were occasional glimpses of the city centre and more recent urban expansion. From there the road took me down the hillside to the southeastern part of Kota Kinabalu, which seemed to be occupied, for the most part, by rundown shopping centres (*kompleks*). Small settlements (*kampungs*) were sited amongst the hillside greenery. I rejoined the city's dual carriageway system that held the various parts of Kota Kinabalu together.

I continued on, a lone walker amongst speeding cars, towards the city centre. By this time it was getting very hot and humid. I passed the sprawling Asia City shopping area, the Kampung Air food market and cafes, via the modest City Park and back into the comparative homely urban form of the Jalan Gaya area with its busy *kedai kopis*.

In the early evening I visited the Suria Sabah, Kota Kinabalu's newest indoor retail centre and a modern contrast to its predominantly rundown shopping facilities. Its four floors of shops and basic restaurants were busy. As I left there was a thunderous rainstorm and, in the sanctuary of a bar close to the hotel, I was told again to be wary of muggers on Jalan Gaya. Despite these dire warnings I didn't experience any threats during my stay.

Accommodation Suggestions (Kota Kinabalu):

Jesselton Hotel (www.jesseltonhotel.com) - a small heritage hotel located on Jalan Gaya in the central Chinatown part of the city.

Hotel Sixty3 (www.hotelsixty3.com) – a bright and modern facility on Jalan Gaya.

Sutera Harbour Resort (www.suteraharbour.com) – five-star resort in Tanjung Aru sited close to Kota Kinabalu's railway station.

North Borneo Railway

DAY 2
Kota Kinabalu to Tenom

Tanjung Aru (Kota Kinabalu)
(Scheduled Departure 0745)
to Beaufort *(Scheduled Arrival 0940)*

Ticket Cost: Ringgit 4.80 or US$1.5 in Economy Class

The taxi left the hotel to the early morning sounds of birds chirping in Jalan Gaya's trees as we drove through the city centre's gridiron streets. We then sped along the dual carriageway to the sounds of Lady Gaga played by the Muslim taxi driver. Tanjung Aru station is very close to the airport, and adjoining it was a construction site for the 'Aeropod' development. Skies were overcast and there were occasional drops of rain with distant dark clouds threatening worse to come.

The small station has three platforms and a modest food court. The waiting area was already quite full and an orderly queue formed to buy tickets, which could not be bought in advance. When I got my ticket to Beaufort I was told the disappointing news that the connecting train to Tenom would not be running. It was *'rusak'* (broken) with engine problems. The Beaufort to Tenom line has a reputation for being plagued with operational difficulties, due to

mechanical or natural reasons (principally landslips following heavy rainfall). Today it was the turn of mechanical challenges.

Tanjung Aru Station

Roughly 70 passengers gathered on Tanjung Aru's small platform to the background noise of aircraft taking off. A Sabah State Railways (SSR) train stood next to a North Borneo Heritage train. The latter is a tourist service operated jointly by SSR and Sutera Harbour Resort that started in 2000 to commemorate Kota Kinabalu's newly granted city status. These trains, with five carriages, are pulled by a Vulcan steam locomotive (built in Manchester in 1954) and run from Tanjung Aru to Papar, roughly half way along the route to Beaufort, and then return to Kota Kinabalu. Carriages are painted in the green and cream livery of the original North Borneo Railway with traditional interior design to reflect décor of the early 1900s. Train attendants are dressed in white uniforms and pith helmets. Passengers are served breakfast on the

outbound trip and 'traditional tiffin' on the way back at a cost of Ringgit 290 (US$90).

Construction of the North Borneo Railway began in 1896. It was built by workers brought in from Japan and was originally intended for transporting tobacco from the interior for export. The first section of 32kms was built to connect Beaufort south to the port of Weston. This was then extended with 48kms of track to Tenom in 1905 with another line added a year later from Tenom northwards to Melalap (16kms). At the same time, work began on another section from Beaufort to Kota Kinabalu, which was completed in 1903 and mostly followed the coastline. The completed routes amounted to 193kms of track. However, during WWII the network was almost entirely destroyed. In 1945, the Australian army set about rebuilding the railway and it was reopened in 1949. It was then decided to axe the Weston branch line in 1963, and in 1970 the Melalap extension from Tenom was also closed to traffic. In 1974 the track was cut back a few kilometres from Kota Kinabalu to Tanjung Aru. In 2007 the entire line was closed for maintenance and repair until it reopened in February 2011.

The three-carriage passenger train to Beaufort pulled in from one of the sidings. It was very much a commuter style train with basic but comfortable seats and fierce air conditioning. The carriage windows were thoughtfully wiped as we waited for departure. We left on time and followed the dual carriageway road corridor that ran alongside the airport and its runway. I was the only foreigner on the train, which was more than half full by the time we left.

Papar Area Landscape

Malay uses a number of English words with altered spelling, thus *stesen, bas, teksi, tiket* and *kaunter*. This, on the face of it makes traveling for English-speaking foreigners appear relatively easy. However, outside of Kota Kinabalu it was clear that English was not well understood and some simple Malay terms proved to be useful for getting around.

Most of the passengers were part of large family groups, with almost all the women wearing *hijabs*. A few men wore *songkok* caps (traditional Malay headwear). There was lively chatter and, once the train left Tanjung Aru, food in foam packaging was brought out. Everyone seemed to be eating except for me. The first stop was Putatan on the outskirts of Kota Kinabalu,

North Borneo Railway

where passengers filled the train leaving standing room only. This was a popular local service.

We traveled through more of Kota Kinabalu's characterless suburbs. Warehouses, garages and supermarkets passed by, generally on the coastal side of the railway line. To the east, green hills rose up in the distance, shrouded by cloud. The train horn blared (almost in celebration) as it left the urban area and passed villages on coastal inlets with stilted wooden houses. We then pulled away from the coast and into the low hills covered in forest or thick vegetation. By this time passengers had finished eating and were busily taking smart phone photos of each other, all accompanied by much giggling. At Kinarut more people got on with many standing. The general atmosphere was one of jollity, almost as if it were a holiday jaunt.

After Kinarut the scenery was more rural with forest, scrub vegetation and plantations, and fewer villages. A buffalo lumbered away and a bright blue kingfisher flitted from tree to telephone wire as the train passed. The first large timber yard came into view. The ticket collector passed through the carriage and didn't bother to check my ticket. Nevertheless, I asked about the Tenom train to see whether he could provide some official insight as to whether it would run – 'maybe yes, maybe no', was the report.

The train stopped at Kawang station, after which were mangrove swamps and villages with brightly painted houses, some stilted. We then crossed a broad river into Papar, an important market town with much passenger activity off and onto the train. The holiday atmosphere continued and there were ironic 'oooohs' as we passed through a short tunnel or crossed a broad river. The smell of tiger balm pervaded the air as aches and pains set in. Photo taking and settling down to adjust or delete the photos just taken continued unabated.

Kimanis Bay Beach

Papar is known as a rice cultivation area in Sabah and whilst there were some rice paddies the prevailing scene was of scrub vegetation and date palm plantations. When we left the town the train followed the coastline of Kimanis Bay, running alongside a sandy beach, with views across glass-calm water. There was a large oil terminal and refinery with its flare burning, as well as timber yards. After Bongawan, a small village with a simple station, much of

the landscape seemed to be in a state of re-growth after forest 'harvesting'. By the time we arrived in Membakut, one of the larger towns on the journey, there was Malay music playing from a radio in the carriage.

Wide Eyed Passenger

A mother with a young two or three-year old boy got on and sat down in front of me. The boy was wearing a fluffy pink 'Angry Bird' cap (on back to front) and looked out of the window wide-eyed at the passing scenery. There was sugar cane cutting in one field and a bright red and yellow Chinese temple. Our imminent arrival at Beaufort was heralded by the train blaring its horn, as well as by more last minute photo taking, this time in groups.

Beaufort is the terminus of this stretch of the North Borneo Line. We arrived on time and disembarked to be greeted by a mangy dog on the platform. Alongside was the small rickety-looking train to Halogilat, a halfway point to Tenom where passengers have to change trains. My 'double-checking' inquiries as to whether there was any train departing towards Tenom were met with shrugs, laughter and 'maybes'. Local passengers were also wondering whether there would be any service, but eventually gave up and walked away. The bad news was confirmed when I asked at the ticket counter. Engine failure was the definitive reason. Should I give up and get the train back to Tanjung Aru at 1100am, wait in the station for a possible train at 1330 to Tenom, or just get a taxi to Tenom?

I decided to take a taxi to Tenom and hoped that there would be a train from Tenom to Beaufort the next day. A taxi driver in the station car park agreed to take me to Tenom for Ringgit 100 (US$32). We drove off along a coast road southwestwards towards Brunei at some speed. Villages of brightly coloured stilted houses flashed by. We passed through Sipitang, a coastal resort for locals and Bruneians, close to the border and then took a left turn into the hills towards Tenom. The distance from Beaufort to Tenom was an indirect 100kms (with Beaufort to Sipitang taking up 30kms). Driving continued at breakneck speed along a broad but winding road, with tyres screeching - I occasionally wondered whether we would make it. In

Tenom Road

these circumstances having an accident or not is just a matter of pure luck.

The Tenom road sometimes broadened out to three carriageways' width. There was little traffic on it except for timber lorries and it became clear that they had caused significant damage to the surface with certain road sections completely denuded of tarmac. The scenery was mostly rural and hilly all the way to Tenom, with occasional date and banana plantations but predominantly forested. Much of the forest appeared to be recovering from felling with stripped patches on the hillside.

As we wound speedily up and down hills there were distant views of the expanse of green scenery with clouds covering some of the hilltops close to Tenom. I asked to stop for a photo, which displeased the driver, who had been grumpy and unhelpful during what little conversation we had. By the time we approached Tenom he wanted to make a stop of his own, this time at his home 'for five minutes'. 'Don't worry', he said. We turned off the main road and into a hamlet to his wooden stilt house, which was set within a palm oil plantation. He thoughtfully left the car's engine and air conditioning on.

When we arrived in Tenom I suggested we stop at the railway station. He seemed unenthused. I asked him how far the station was from the Hotel Perkasa. He flicked two fingers at me. I decided to just get to the hotel, as clearly we had had enough of each other. The car climbed up the steep forested approach road to the hotel, which stood alone on a hilltop with scenic views over Tenom town and the valley below. The driver got out of the car and nonchalantly lifted open the car boot and left me to get my bag out. This was the last straw and I decided he had foregone any prospects of a tip.

The Hotel Perkasa Tenom was rundown but the only realistic option in town. The scenic views over the valley below provided some compensation. Everything else was grim, including the fried rice offering in its lobby café. The premises were seriously in need of refurbishment or, even better, demolition and a restart. I ate my fried rice while a group of three men were seated nearby discussing a property project. One was uniformed with a 'Malaysia1' shirt and probably a municipality officer. The developer, who was complaining about electricity problems, spoke deferentially to him.

Tenom is a medium-sized town with a population of roughly 50,000, mostly mixed indigenous inhabitants (principally Murut, as well as Kadazan-Dusun, Lun and other groups) and also some Chinese and Malay. The Chinese were drawn to Tenom from Guangdong Province to farm its fertile soil. During the British colonial period it was known as Fort Birch. There was a brief Murut uprising against British rule, known as the Rundum Revolt, led by Ontoros Antonom, whose statue is in the town centre.

Later in the afternoon I decided to look around Tenom and perhaps, just maybe, establish what the prospects were for a train to Beaufort the next day. I followed the road down the forested slopes and took a stick with me in case I met a pack of stray dogs that I'd seen near the hotel. I wandered through the drab centre to the railway station, where I learned that there would be no train that day, but there may be one the following morning if they could repair the engine. I returned to the hotel and on the way back bought some pot noodles for 'dinner'. I could still taste the grease from lunch and was determined not to have any more hotel food. The rest of the afternoon and evening was spent in my grubby room.

Accommodation Suggestions (Tenom):

Hotel Perkasa Tenom (www. perkasahotel.com.my) - the only option in Tenom with attractive views over the valley.

North Borneo Railway

DAY 3
Tenom to Kota Kinabalu

Tenom *(Scheduled Departure 0730)*
to Beaufort *(Scheduled Arrival 0950)*

Ticket Cost: Ringgit 2.55 or US$0.80 in Economy Class

Beaufort *(Scheduled Departure 1100)*
to Tanjung Aru (Kota Kinabalu)
(Scheduled Arrival 1310)

Ticket Cost: Ringgit 4.80 or US$1.50 in Economy Class

I woke up early, in order to try to determine whether there would indeed be a train in the morning or not and, if not, whether there would be one in the afternoon. This was starting to get obsessive. I was also keen to leave the Hotel Perkasa and its grim accommodation as soon as possible. One negative portent was that there had been heavy rain the night before so I prepared for the worst. The hotel staff tried hard to find out for me by phoning both Beaufort and Tenom stations at regular intervals. Beaufort station did finally answer to inform that there would be a scheduled service in the morning. I could barely contain my joy.

The hotel receptionist who did the telephoning kindly offered to take me to the station. As we drove off the morning was cloudy and overcast. We arrived as the ticket office opened and, sure enough, tickets were actually being sold. My jubilation was complete. The receptionist refused to take any money from me for his efforts and embodied a beacon of light at an otherwise dismal establishment. Soon after he left, the train appeared from covered sidings and rattled its way noisily alongside the platform. Much inspecting of the engine by railway staff followed and debates ensued as to its health. Doubt suddenly emerged and the suspense was prolonged. Finally, the discussion group dispersed amidst laughter and passengers were released onto the platform in jovial mood. There was a strong degree of theatre about all this.

Tenom Station and the Halogilat Train

The train had two tinny freight carriages with no windows and a couple of benches bolted to the thin metal sides. Otherwise, there were sliding doors that were left open.

There was a very rudimentary passenger carriage.   Luckily, for photographic purposes, windows and doors were left open. The carriage was full mostly with children that had all the appearance of being on a holiday excursion. I was the only foreigner in the carriage.

We pulled out of Tenom station to much fanfare of blaring horns. The sun broke out from behind the clouds. How symbolic! Off we went chugging and jolting along as the engine dragged the three carriages out. With this much-heralded departure a woman immediately handed out lollipops to all the children. The ticket collector came to check tickets and as mine was being inspected there seemed to be a freezing of action from the kids who stared at me and then, once the ticket was given back and all was well, returned to their lollipops almost with palpable relief. Food was then brought out and the serious eating started.

The train followed a brownish fast flowing river, the Padas, and the line hugged a steep-sided part of the valley with slopes covered in thick forest.   Cloud and mist swirled about.   The back door of the carriage was kept open and passengers peered at the railway line disappearing behind us. The carriages rattled and rocked their way slowly alongside the river. We passed a small dam and hydroelectric plant, after which the river rushed and frothed alongside. There were few houses, just forest.

Between Pangi and Rayoh

The first station, Pangi, adjoined a whitewater rafting resort. Dozens of rafters in wet suits suddenly ran out and funneled into the freight carriages. Not all could fit in and some had to wait until the next train in the early afternoon. Soon after we left the station the train lurched to a brief grinding halt, as rocks were cleared away from the track. Landslip evidence was everywhere. The steep-sided rock face passed by at an arms length away from the carriage. Small waterfalls gushed down the rocks and splashed water through the open window. The train continued to grind and creak its way along the track at jogging pace. Carriage metal doors crashed and banged. Passengers had stopped eating and were staring out at the passing scenery.

North Borneo Railway

Friendly Rayoh Station Dogs

We arrived at Rayoh station to be greeted by a group of five tail-wagging stray dogs. The whitewater rafters got out and off we went at a slow rocking amble alongside the broadening river, passing teams of construction workers clearing landslip damage and repairing the track. In one section the riverbank had been completely rebuilt and the track recently replaced. In 2008 one section of the line had disintegrated and train carriages had fallen into the river below killing two passengers. We picked up speed and passed more stilted houses and some cultivation, including pineapple growing plots. One-and-a-half hours after leaving Tenom we arrived in Halogilat station, the halfway point to Beaufort. Crowds of passengers were waiting to take this train back towards Tenom, many in wet suits.

Once out and on to the platform passengers from Tenom had to immediately get onto a Beaufort-bound train, which waited at the same platform. It was an exact copy of the train we had left. Five minutes later it slowly pulled out of the station and soon picked up speed with carriages banging together as the pace changed. A snack and drinks seller had joined us and did a brisk business. We stopped at Saliwangan station, next to which was a neat school and grass playground. The terrain flattened out with low hills and the river widened. There were banana and date palm plantations and more houses. Halts became increasingly numerous at tiny settlements. The train shuddered and jolted along as it descended towards Beaufort. At one village stop a tarmac road suddenly appeared, which we followed to Beaufort and relative civilisation. In the distance an aggregate mining area and hillsides cleared of forest came into view.

We arrived at Beaufort station roughly on time. There was still an hour before the next train would leave for Tanjung Aru, perfectly timed for me to get some food. Just across from the station was a pleasant cafe (Old Town Little Cafe) which had some framed photos of Beaufort and the North Borneo Railway from the 1940s and 1950s: Beaufort Theatre, old steam engines, a former government rest house and images of flooding.

I got back to the station and the waiting Kota Kinabalu train, which was now almost full. A young girl in a *hijab* smiled sweetly at me (later, she asked where I was from).

Padas River from Rayoh Station

Carriage air conditioning saved everyone from the 32°C temperatures outside. As we departed, passengers brought out their lunch on cue. Flooded areas passed by on the outskirts of Beaufort. At Membakut more passengers got on with standing room only left. The carriage started to heat up. Although the coastal towns appeared to be mostly drab, there were some interesting terraces of town centre wooden shops. The train continued to fill up after Bongawan. When we arrived at Tanjung Aru station passengers flocked to waiting minibuses (*bas persiaran*), which took them to the town centre bus station. One of the station security guards helpfully rang for a taxi for me and within twenty minutes I was back in Jalan Gaya.

An evening walk along the promenade from the Suria Sabah shopping centre, via the Hyatt Regency and along the waterfront, took me past a multitude of outdoor stalls and tables with fish-grilling sending up clouds of smoke. The smell of fish being cooked masked the stench of sewage, which wafted up from the sea. The tide was also bringing in carpets of plastic and wooden detritus to the promenade wall. Another market selling cheap goods was shutting up as I went by. There were more outdoor food stalls before reaching a waterside row of restaurants and bars ('Cock and Bull', 'Down Under Aussie Bar' and the 'Shamrock Irish Bar').

DAY 4
Kota Kinabalu

The Likas Wetland Reserve (or Kota Kinabalu Wetland Centre) is roughly two kilometres north of the city centre. The taxi took me along a dual carriageway route around Jesselton Point and alongside Likas Bay, which opened out with attractive views across the water to a backdrop of green mountains. The large and distinctive Kota Kinabalu City Mosque was clearly visible in the distance.

low tide) as small dark crabs busied away. The sun glinted through the trees and the exposed forest of raised roots provided a curious 'other world' environment. A variety of wildlife can be seen including egrets and wading birds, owls and eagles, kingfishers, monitor lizards as well as dog-faced water snakes. What I actually saw in a 45-minute circuit along boardwalks was the occasional squirrel, kingfisher, skink and egret. A lot of plastic rubbish lurked around tree roots. The best time to visit would probably have been early morning or during dusk.

Sabah State Mosque and Mount Kinabalu in the Background

Likas Wetlands Reserve

The Wetland Centre was opened in 2000 and is protected by the World Wildlife Fund. There are 24 hectares of fresh water mangrove that form a migratory stopping point for birds from as far away as Siberia. The walk through the mangrove forest was cool and shaded with a symphony of popping from the exposed mud (it was

I walked back to Jalan Gaya along the Likas Bay waterfront promenade and past the Jesselton Point port area. Much of the port had been cleared and was due to be developed with apartments, a conference centre and shops, all alluringly advertised as being eco-friendly with seductive photos of Sabah's natural environment. On top of

Likas Bay Fisherman

Tanjung Aru Stilted Village

Pacific Sutera Hotel Beach

the slopes that looked down on the port were modern high-rise apartment blocks.

Later, I took a taxi to Tanjung Aru and the Sutera Harbour Resort. It was scorchingly hot by this time. We approached through the resort's gateway and along an attractively landscaped boulevard, flanked by golf courses. There were two hotel complexes with a marina sandwiched between them. The marina jetty had large boats from Malta and the West Indies. The sun was beating down. No one was swimming in

the sea next to the beach probably because the water was not particularly clean. It was awash with floating plastic and wood. A net was strung along the private beach entrance and a pool attendant was picking up rubbish washed up on the sand. By the time he'd finished, more detritus had been quickly delivered by the waves. Swimming in the sea was not an enticing prospect. I returned to the hotel's lobby area to the sounds of 'What a Wonderful World' from a singer-pianist.

I then ventured out on to the golf course. I wanted to take in the view of the coastal *kampung* stilt houses opposite the resort. The weather had changed and was increasingly overcast, as I skirted golf buggies and the odd golf ball that seemed to bounce from nowhere. From the shoreline the view of the stilted *kampung* provided a jumbled multi-coloured contrast to the manicured greens of the golf course.

West Coast
Peninsular Malaysia

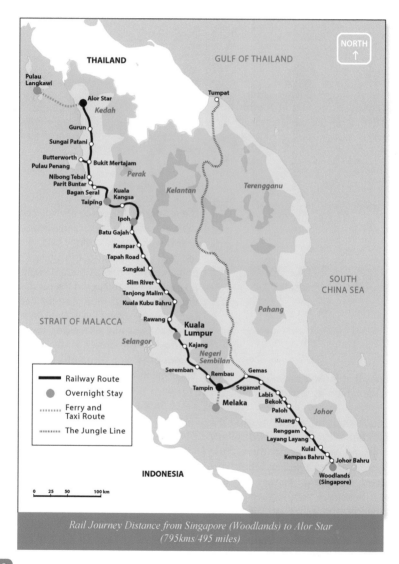

NORTH
↑

THAILAND

GULF OF THAILAND

Pulau Langkawi

Alor Star

Kedah

Tumpat

Gurun

Sungai Patani

Butterworth
Pulau Penang

Bukit Mertajam

Perak

Nibong Tebal
Parit Buntar

Bagan Seral

Kuala Kangsa

Kelantan

Terengganu

Taiping

Ipoh

Batu Gajah

Kampar

Tapah Road

Sungkal

Slim River

Tanjong Malim

Kuala Kubu Bahru

STRAIT OF MALACCA

Rawang

Kuala Lumpur

Selangor

Kajang

Negeri Sembilan

SOUTH CHINA SEA

Pahang

Seremban

Rembau

Gemas

Tampin

Segamat

Labis

Bekok

Melaka

Paloh

Johor

Kluang

Renggam

Layang Layang

Kulal

Kempas Bahru

Johor Bahru

INDONESIA

Woodlands (Singapore)

▬▬	Railway Route
●	Overnight Stay
········	Ferry and Taxi Route
▪▪▪▪▪▪▪	The Jungle Line

0   25   50   100 km

*Rail Journey Distance from Singapore (Woodlands) to Alor Star
(795kms/495 miles)*

West Coast Peninsular Malaysia:
Singapore to Alor Star (and Langkawi)

I always felt lucky on a train, as on this one. So many other travelers are hurrying to the airport, to be interrogated and frisked and their luggage searched for bombs. They would be better off on a national railway, probably the best way of getting a glimpse of how people actually live – the back garden, the barns, the hovels, the side roads and slums, the telling facts of village life, the misery that aeroplanes fly over. Yes, the train takes more time, and many trains are dirty, but so what? Delay and dirt are the realities of the most rewarding travel.

– Paul Theroux from 'Ghost Train To The Eastern Star' (2008)

Keretapi Tanah Melayu (KTM) operates Malaysia's railway system. Travel by train through Peninsular Malaysia is comfortable and convenient. There is one main operational railway line running through this part of the country. This follows the western side from Padang Besar via Kuala Lumpur to Johor Bahru and Singapore, which is being upgraded with electrification and double-tracking works to enable train speeds of 160kph. It's also proposed to build a high-speed rail link from Kuala Lumpur to Singapore.

A second line ('The Jungle Line') extends from Gemas (in the south west) through the middle of the peninsular to Tumpat and Kota Bahru on the northeastern coast, where there are connections to Sungai Kolok (and thereafter Hat Yai) in Thailand.

However, this route was badly damaged following flooding in late 2014 and will be out of service during the next two years for repair works.

KTM trains have first and second-class seating and overnight sleeper accommodation in air conditioned carriages. There is also a 'deluxe sleeping' carriage with one or two-bed private rooms (with toilet and shower) on overnight trains from Singapore to Kuala Lumpur. The website for KTM is partly available in English (www.ktmb.com.my) where advance tickets can be obtained online. Tickets can be bought easily at railway stations (where English is widely spoken), although during public holidays it is advisable to buy tickets with some notice.

West Coast Peninsular Malaysia

DAY 1
Singapore to Pulau Sebang/ Tampin

Singapore Woodlands Checkpoint Station (*Scheduled Departure 0830*) **to Pulau Sebang/Tampin** (*Scheduled Arrival 1342*). Ekspres Rakyat

Ticket Cost: Singapore$25 or US$33 in AFC Premier Class Reserved Seats

A taxi ride through Singapore's early morning darkness took me to the imposing Woodlands Train Checkpoint building (also known as Woodlands CIQ) on the island state's northern coast. By the time I got there it was bright sunshine but unfortunately I'd arrived much too early. A long queue had already formed across a pedestrian bridge into the immigration building and railway station. I needed to kill some time so wandered around a nearby municipally-designed market and food court area, complete with concrete planters and a convoluted network of routes paved in red brick. It reminded me of 1970's Britain and was very unlike present day Singapore. I was approached twice by helpful Singaporeans and told how to get to Woodlands Train Checkpoint building without even asking. Clearly, foreign visitors had struggled to find their way through this municipal maze to get the train to Malaysia. I returned and joined the queue on the bridge where we were kept waiting until 15 minutes before the train's departure. There were no cafes or cooled waiting rooms. This was rudimentary and very unlike the experience of Tanjong Pagar Station in central Singapore where, until four years ago, trains started their journey into Malaysia.

Everyone stood in the queue sweltering, cooled only by an occasional overhead fan. People arriving from Malaysia walked by. I could also see a stream of motorbikes passing through immigration controls. The train to Malaysia waited at the platform

Kluang Station

Woodlands Checkpoint is one of two physical crossing points from Singapore into Malaysia and one of the busiest border crossings in the world. Every day some 50,000 people travel along the Causeway and across the short width of the Johore Strait from Johor Bahru into Singapore. The second designated crossing point from Singapore to Malaysia is to the west at Tuas. Woodlands Train Checkpoint has been the southern terminus of the KTM Intercity service since July 2011. This followed an agreement between Malaysia and Singapore to close Tanjong Pagar railway station in central Singapore. At Woodlands Train Checkpoint northbound passengers clear both Singapore Immigration and Malaysian Customs and Immigration before boarding the train for Malaysia, while southbound passengers clear Malaysian Immigration at Johor Bahru Sentral Station and then Singapore Customs and Immigration at Woodlands.

However, in July 2015 (after this trip was undertaken), a shuttle train service (Shuttle Tebrau) connects Woodlands Train Checkpoint across the Causeway to Johor Bahru Sentral Station. This means that KTM Intercity train services that previously linked Woodlands with stations in Malaysia have now been terminated at Johor Bahru Sentral. Thus, railway passengers from Singapore must first get the shuttle train to Johor Bahru Sentral before connecting with the KTM Intercity train.

A high-speed rail link is also planned to connect Kuala Lumpur to the western part of Singapore with seven stops along its 340km route. The cost of the line is estimated to be US$30 billion and will cut the journey time to 90 minutes. The operational date is likely to be 2026.

below us. Once we were allowed into the station, clearance through Singapore passport control and then Malaysian immigration and customs (who were in adjacent rooms in the building) was quick. The message is don't arrive too early at Woodlands otherwise the wait will be tedious and uncomfortable. Also, don't take photos in the station.

Only one other person was in my first class carriage, which was in need of a thorough clean and, ideally, an upgrade. The train pulled out gently about ten minutes late and we rattled along the Johore Strait Causeway, past traffic queuing into Singapore. A couple of minutes later we were in Johor Bahru's Sentral Station where, after a short wait in the station's enclosed, dark and empty gloom, we were on our way again. We passed a Hindu temple, tired and worn looking hotels and shopping centres, occasional high-rise apartment blocks, graveyards and shanty settlements. From this perspective Johor Bahru did not encourage a visit.

I'd eaten little and was starving. The buffet car was next door. After a first visit I was told to return in half an hour. We passed the small ramshackle station of Kempas Bahru,

West Coast Peninsular Malaysia

where there was evidence of railway track improvement. Double track upgrading of Malaysia's main railway line has been in progress since my first long distance railway trip through Malaysia in early 2011 (as part of the Bangkok to Singapore journey). Eventually, and despite indifferent service delivered to a fine art, I did manage to get some food. Even though the *nasi goreng* (fried rice) was distinctly unappetising, I still had two portions such was the extent of my hunger. Next time, however, I would be bringing my own food onto the train. When I returned from the buffet car a bottle of water and a piece of banana cake had been placed on my seat.

Kluang Area Landscape

I'd been talking to a UK traveler, Tim, who was in his late sixties and had been living in San Francisco for 30 years. He was taking a sabbatical from IT work to travel around the world, principally by boat and train. He would be staying in Georgetown (Penang) for a few days. He told me he'd recently returned to the UK to visit his mother who was now 92. She had remarried at 90 (to another nonagenarian) after the death of her husband, and would be flying to the US for his son's wedding. When the train made a station stop Tim would leap off in search of food and then quickly return clutching a bun, such was the buffet car offering.

We passed a landscape of mostly palm oil plantations and forest, with isolated hills in the distance, as well as rows of newly developed housing units. The train stopped at stations of small and drab towns, such as Layang Layang, where mosques were the grandest of the buildings. On one station platform a large portly man stood in a white sari stroking his long hair and looking blankly into the middle distance. There was bright sunshine by now and the carriage air conditioning was working its thankful magic.

The train ambled along and speeded up only where there was double tracking. Railway improvements were in full swing at the large and modern Gemas Station, a junction for 'The Jungle Line' to the northeastern corner of Malaysia. Tim, saw an opportunity for more station food and took his chances again. The next station, Pulau Sebang/Tampin, was a copy of Gemas, and was where I got off to go to Melaka (Malacca). The station was largely empty with little evidence of passengers or railway staff.

Bekok Station Shop Houses

I found a taxi driver, hovering outside the station in a largely deserted car park, who would take me to Melaka. He was in his late sixties, wore a batik shirt, black *songkok* (traditional Malay headwear) and sunglasses. His car was in bad shape and it was no wonder that he kept it tucked away when negotiating. He closed his window with both hands gripping on to the glass. The engine spluttered into life and it was soon clear that the air conditioning didn't work either, on this most blistering of days. The distance to Melaka was 38kms and he kept up a continuous chatter, which built up to tours that he could do, as well as other marketing attempts. From what I could glean in his rapidly heating car, as the sun beat down on the back of my neck, he had two wives, ten children and 35 grandchildren. He planned to retire soon and would then embark on another *haj*, he said. He banged the steering wheel to emphasise his points and continued talking. Another driver irritated him: 'You no give road me, I give road. You no give road.' He was also in the habit of expressing not so subtle anti-Chinese sentiments. As we got closer to Melaka the hard sell was being ramped up. We finally arrived at my hotel, the Majestic, after I had been fully roasted. The driver had no change, of course, so I went into the hotel. He followed and cheekily took some sweets from a jar on the counter. I give him what we agreed and he stood there staring at the money. I walked off, adamant that I would not be tipping him for that taxi experience. An American couple was waiting in the hotel lobby. I had briefly chatted to them in the Tampin Station lift and we joked about the state of my taxi compared to their infinitely more comfortable car.

Pulau Sebang/Tampin Station

During the 15th Century Melaka was a key port in South East Asia and one of the earliest Malay sultanates, initially founded by a Sumatran Hindu Prince. It was a centre for the spice trade attracting Arab, Tamil and Chinese merchants, and later colonised initially by the Portuguese in 1511 and

then by the Dutch and British. The Dutch formally ceded Melaka to the British in 1824 in exchange for the Sumatran port of Bengkulu. Melaka then formed part of the Straits Settlements, together with Penang, Dinding and Singapore. However, the importance of the port town declined with the rise of Singapore. It's now one of the largest cities in Malaysia with a population of 860,000 and is characterised by a diverse mixture of ethnicities. In 2008 the centre of Melaka was granted UNESCO World Heritage Site status and the number of visitors to the city grew rapidly thereafter.

Melaka Majestic Hotel Tea Set

The Majestic Hotel is located on the River Melaka, which winds through the city. This heritage hotel is split into two buildings. The original 1920's former colonial mansion has been restored and includes the reception area with a beautifully tiled floor and quiet library room. A new ten-storey colonial-style addition sits at the back and has rooms with teak wooden floors.

I decided to take a riverside walk towards the city centre and Chinatown and followed a boardwalk past an enormous shopping mall, hotel and apartments ('The Shore') that formed a towering modern landmark for the city. It presented a stark contrast to Kampung Morten, just across the river, an area of traditional one-storey housing, including stilt structures, the best known being Villa Sentosa. It was a wonderful route along the winding river and had a very Dutch feel to it with buildings pressing in onto the canalised river.

The route changed from boardwalk to footpath with lights picking out trees, flowers and murals on the backs of buildings, typically of a pirate and swashbuckling theme. There were cafes and bars along the riverside. After a half-hour walk I was in Chinatown with its narrow one-way streets of tightly packed shop houses (Jalan Hang Jebat, Jonker Street and Jalan Tun Tan Cheng Lock). By this time streets were quiet albeit with occasional shops, restaurants and workshops open. I passed one workshop with its shutter doors ajar and the incongruous sight of pig carcasses being cut up.

Accommodation Suggestions (Melaka):

Majestic Hotel (www.majesticmalacca. com) - heritage hotel on the River Melaka and close to the centre of the city.

DAY 2
Melaka

The day started overcast but soon the sky cleared and temperatures rose. I crossed the road from the hotel and walked through Kampung Morten past its attractive traditional houses under the looming modern tower that is The Shore. The riverside route had a very different feel during the day from the previous evening, less atmospheric and harsher thanks to the rising temperatures. I passed 'Pirate Park' and its companion mini version of the 'London Eye' wheel. During daytime the changes in character along the route were more stark as one moved from a landscaped environment with trees and reeds to urban surroundings with buildings pressing in on the riverside.

By the time I got to the Stadthuys and the St Paul's Hill area I had to get away from the beating sun and find somewhere cool - temperatures were up to 35C° with little breeze. Refuge was found in one of the larger hotels, the Casa del Rio that

Riverside Buildings

West Coast Peninsular Malaysia

appeared to be a 'Mediterranean design meets Asia' establishment, for a drink in an air conditioned sanctuary.

Chinatown during the day was busy and the narrow streets had almost continuous one-way traffic. There was elaborate detailing on the area's almost intact group of decorative shop houses. Many buildings were in the same state as they were during the 1940's and 1950's, whilst others had been refurbished for guesthouse accommodation, art galleries, cafes and restaurants, shops and small museums. Traditional shops sold herbal medicine, hardware, antiques and tea. There was also a mixture of mosques, Hindu and Buddhist temples.

I crossed the river from Chinatown to the Stadthuys, Melaka's iconic landmark, distinctive for the ochre brown rendered group of buildings. Rickshaws ('cyclos') gathered around shaded areas close to the clock tower. Melaka's cyclos are gaudily decorated, often in pinks and light blues with butterfly covers. At night they could be seen cycling through the empty streets in a blaze of flashing lights and booming music, typically playing crooning Malay ballads.

The Dutch built Stadthuys (town hall) in the 1650s, after taking over from the Portuguese. The buildings were occupied by the Governor of Melaka's office, as well as by the Dutch East Indies Company, up to

The Riverside

River Melaka

Heeren House in Chinatown

1824. The Dutch Governor's residence, and the local prison, were built on the adjoining St Paul's Hill. Stadthuys was constructed with thick brick walls, large windows and doors, with an underground drainage system that flowed into the River Melaka. Buildings were originally painted in white until it was redecorated to its current rich brown colour during the 1820's. When the British took over it continued to operate as an administrative centre for Malaya and, after independence, was Melaka State's government centre until 1979. More recently, renovation work was completed in the late 1980's, since when the Stadthuys has become the centrepiece of the city's UNESCO World Heritage Site.

I went into the Stadthuys' Christ Church, built in 1753, which was decorated simply inside with whitewashed walls, little detailing and no stained glass. One stone plaque on the wall read:

Melaka Cyclo

> 'Beneath this stone is inter'd
> With her still-born infant
> The remains of
> Mrs Mary Betty,
> Who departed this life
> Sept. 20th 1800.
> Aged 30 years.
> Her disconsolate husband
> Has caused this stone to be placed here
> As a small mark of his regard
> For an amiable and affectionate wife'

I thought back to the last time I was in Melaka some 28 years ago. It was a

Stadthuys' Christ Church

Former Melaka Governor's Residence

much quieter place then, a bit more run-down, with fewer visitors but without the improvements such as the riverside route. On top of St. Paul's Hill is the former Governor's residence and next to it the ruined structure of St. Paul's Church. Adjoining the former church walls were a couple of stalls selling tourist memorabilia, which included plastic chickens dangling down from the tarpaulin. When squeezed the chickens gave out a crowing noise. This attracted repeated plastic chicken squeezing by members of an Asian tour group with obligatory photo taking. Everyone in the group seemed obliged to repeat the chicken squeezing to the accompaniment of much laughter.

Stadthuys is the focal point for the wealth of museums in Melaka that includes the Malaysia Youth Museum, Malaysia Democratic Government Museum, Malaysia Arts, Culture and Literature

Museum and the History and Ethnography Museum. The Maritime Museum is also nearby. I followed a path down the hill to the clock tower and then back along the riverside. I'd had enough of being in this heat and headed back to The Shore's air conditioned shopping sanctuary.

Many of the shop houses along the riverside had closed. A monitor lizard lay in the water with its chin propped lazily on a rock. It'd also had enough. In The Shore I stopped off at an ice cream kiosk for a scoop of rum and raisin. The answer was 'we don't have rum and raisin, but we do have raisin'. Regulations had determined that even a minimal amount of alcoholic content in ice cream should be banned.

St. Paul's Church, Melaka

DAY 3
Pulau Sebang/Tampin to Kuala Lumpur

Pulau Sebang/Tampin *(Scheduled Departure 1342)* **to Kuala Lumpur** *(Scheduled Arrival 1609).*
Ekspres Rakyat

Ticket Cost: Ringgit 27 or US$7 in AFC Premier Class Reserved Seats

I took some food from breakfast for the train journey to Kuala Lumpur (KL) rather than risk the railway buffet's food. The weather was overcast and cooler and the taxi to Tampin Station, thankfully, had decent air conditioning and the driver was pleasantly unassertive. As we left Melaka we passed a large Tesco supermarket, as well as rows of bland two-storey shops either empty or under construction that were lined along the main road. These functional structures were a stark contrast to the beautiful traditional one-storey stilt houses that could be seen closer to Tampin. Most were painted in a dark brown, with some in a cream colour. Some houses were on wooden stilts, others on stone pillars and many brightly decorated.

The train from Tampin Station was delayed by half an hour. As I waited I looked at a 'Malaysia Railway Homestay Experience'. poster, which advertised combined

Majestic Hotel Library Room

Villa Sentosa, Kampung Morten

packages of family-run guest house accommodation and rail tickets (*www.malaysiarailwaytourism.weebly.com/experience-malaysian-homestay-by-rail*). There are various packages mostly linked to rural tourism. Alarmingly, however, visitors are 'handed over to foster families'. Shortly before the train arrived we were let through. The station was larger than it needed to be, very much underused, and doubtless awaiting the arrival of the high-

The Shore, Melaka

speed trains in roughly ten years time. At one end of the long platforms was a Hindu temple and at the other a large Buddhist temple.

Soon after leaving Tampin Station the train sped along, now that we were on the upgraded section of track. Forested hills appeared to the east but there were also areas cleared for new development. It started to rain as we entered the large town of Seremban. A commuter train waited on the other platform with women only carriages. Passengers huddled together underneath minimal shelter. A young American couple sitting behind me discussed insurance policies and their investments almost continuously throughout the journey as the countryside flowed past them.

We passed Bangi station and an enormous waterpark. The number of construction sites increased as we approached KL – roads, recent development and also an elevated concrete structure for the high-speed railway. The outskirts of the city had a mix of down-at-heel shopping malls, *kampung* (small settlements) and high-rise public housing. A few minutes later this changed to modern high-rise condominium blocks, large detached houses set around a lake with manicured gardens and glitzy shopping centres. A building site advertised apartments in 'Green Park'. We were getting close to the city centre and then, sure enough, after Salak Selatan Station, views of KL's iconic building, Petronas Towers, came into view. The train rumbled through concrete surroundings and a tunnel as we drew into KL Sentral, a covered and darkened station.

Shortly after we pulled out and only a few hundred metres later the train arrived into Kuala Lumpur Station, the former central station for the city until 2001 when KL Sentral took over this role. However, this station, built in 1910, is still a landmark building in the city. It was designed by AB Hubback and followed an Anglo-Asian Islamic architectural style that can also be seen in other buildings of its time throughout Malaysia. It has distinctive elevated dome-shaped pavilions (*chhatris*) that are typical of traditional Indian architecture in Rajasthan. Since 2001 this large and empty station has been looking

Kuala Lumpur Station

numerous elevated one–way streets. The focal point was of course the Petronas Towers in all its gleaming and glittering stainless steel dominance, spectacularly lit up for a nighttime display. The building was designed by the Argentine-US architect, Cesar Pelli, and took seven years to construct on the site of KL's former race track, the Selangor Turf Club. Not only was it the tallest building in the world when it opened in 1998 (until 2004), but it's still the tallest twin-towered structure in the world. The two towers of 88 floors reach up to 450 metres high with a connecting double decker sky bridge half way up (the highest two-storey bridge in the world).

for new functions to fill its enormous space, other than solely as a commuter station. In 2007 it included a railway museum with exhibits in the main hall and on platforms.

I was one of two or three passengers that got off here and walked through the large steel-framed covered station to the ticket office, where no one was able to sell any onward tickets. I asked the only person sitting in the public area where the ticket official might be. He replied grumpily: 'gone to relax'. The taxi from the station to my hotel seemed to follow a very circuitous route indeed but I was in no position to complain. It was nice just to eventually get into a comfortable hotel room.

In the evening I looked around the Petronas Towers area. Kuala Lumpur City Centre (KLCC) is a mix of high-rise buildings, beautiful trees and parkland, as well as

That evening around the Petronas Towers a selfie and photo-taking frenzy was taking place. Selfie sticks and the 'V' for victory signs were abundant. At its building base is the up-market Suria KLCC shopping centre with the customary high-end branded shops collected inside.

Accommodation Suggestions (Kuala Lumpur):

Impiana KLCC (www.impiana.com. my) - modern four-star hotel in the city centre with infinity pool views of Petronas Towers.

Majestic Hotel (www.majestickl.com) - five-star heritage hotel located opposite Kuala Lumpur Station.

West Coast Peninsular Malaysia

DAY 4
Kuala Lumpur

The next morning I started off through KLCC's main park with its lakes and attractive trees, many of which were impressive *banyans*. The large open space was encircled by high-rise apartments, hotels, offices, a conference centre and, of course, the Petronas Towers and Suria shopping mall. As I passed the base of the

KLCC Park

Petronas Towers to get to KLCC Light Rail Transit (LRT) Station the selfie photo taking was still in progress, a continuous day and night activity. I took the LRT three stops down the line to Masjid Jamek Station for Chinatown. The attractive Masjid Jamek mosque could be seen as I emerged from the station with its white cupolas, as well as the shiny copper-plated domes of the Sultan Abdul Samad Building in Merdeka Square just beyond it. I negotiated my way along the maze of walkways and was just

Petronas Towers

Masjid Jamek

about to reach street level, when I asked two girls in *hijabs* in which direction I should go to get to Chinatown. They didn't have a clue. The area was very close but, clearly, their lives didn't take them to Chinatown. Once outside into the busy streets I passed through a Muslim food market, packed with a lunchtime crowd, and then on to Old Market Square. This area was full of money transfer and exchange outlets with mostly South Asians sending remittences back home, probably earned on building sites.

Chinatown Shop Houses

Chinatown has a mix of heritage and not so old buildings, generally in poor shape and covered in advertising signs. A few

buildings, mostly shop houses, have been refurbished and repainted in bright colours, the oldest originating from the early 1900's. Petaling Street is the main focus for visitors to Chinatown and is covered by a canopy along a busy street market selling mostly t-shirts, cheap handbags and shoes. A walk through it will attract hustling attempts from mostly South Asian sellers. The area has a seedy and grim atmosphere to it, with little charm. The traffic-clogged streets don't help much either. There are beggars and street sleepers aplenty. It's not a pleasant place to spend much time in. As one moves towards the southern end of Petaling Street, the real Chinatown starts to emerge with shop houses occupied by merchants and offices. I continued though narrow streets past temples and workshops to a landscaped roundabout on Jalan Maharajalela where there was a large Buddhist temple and the distinctive white Chinese Assembly Hall.

Guan Di Temple Figures, Chinatown

West Coast Peninsular Malaysia

Kuala Lumpur ('muddy confluence' in Malay) is Malaysia's national capital and largest city with a population of 1.6 million. Greater KL, which extends into the Klang Valley, has one of the fastest growing populations in South East Asia at 7.5 million. Although KL is also the country's parliamentary seat and official residence of the Malaysian King, the executive and judicial branches of the federal government have moved to Putrajaya since 1999. KL is still the cultural and financial centre of Malaysia and one of three federal territories in the country, which forms an administrative enclave within the state of Selangor.

The city's origins emerged from tin mining during the second half of the 19th Century, principally from the Ampang mines, which attracted southern Chinese prospectors and labour. The early period of KL's growth was plagued by disease, flooding and fires, as well as destruction during the Selangor Civil War. As a consequence, the British colonial administration determined that a new KL be built, mostly in brick and tile. This started a brick industry (hence the Brickfields area in the central part of the city) and the construction of new buildings resembling those in southern China, originally called 'five foot ways' and more commonly known as shop houses, which are a typical feature of colonial architecture in this part of Asia. A railway line built between KL and Klang in 1886 led to a fourfold increase in the population to 20,000 by 1890. In 1896 KL became the capital of the newly formed Federated Malay States. From those early days a mix of different communities settled in various parts of the city with the Chinese close to the commercial centre, in what is now Chinatown, and the Malays, Indian Chettiars and Indian Muslims living along Java Street (now Jalan Tun Perak). The Padang, currently Merdeka Square, was the British administrative centre.

The Japanese occupied KL from January 1942 to August 1945, during which time the city continued to grow with the production of rubber and tin. Soon after the Japanese left, the country was preoccupied with the communist insurgency. In 1957, the Federation of Malaya gained its independence from British rule and Malaysia was subsequently formed in September 1963, throughout which time KL remained as the capital. In May 1969 the city was shaken by the worst race riots on record between the Malay and Chinese communities, with almost 200 people killed. Rioting was sparked by Malay dissatisfaction with their socio-political status and led to the promotion of Malay economic development over other ethnic groups.

I wanted to walk to the nearby Majestic Hotel, opposite Kuala Lumpur Station. It was probably no more than 300 metres away but the myriad of flyovers and dual carriageway roads meant that it would be impenetrable for a pedestrian, so I capitulated and got a taxi. This resulted in a journey of about five times the distance of what could have been a direct route, as we sped along dual carriageways did a u-turn and back in the opposite direction before u-turning again to reach the Majestic Hotel. We probably passed it, or came very close to it, twice before finally arriving there.

It was a much grander affair than the Majestic in Melaka. I was greeted by a hotel doorman dressed in a white colonial outfit and took myself off to a quiet tucked-away place in the lobby to cool off (and dry out) in the air-conditioning. I felt awkward in this unkempt state and went to the garden terrace and looked out at the whitewashed *chhatris* of Kuala Lumpur Station. Opposite the station is the very similarly designed Railway Administration Building.

The Hotel Majestic was built in 1932 in a mix of neo-classical and art deco styles with many fixtures and fittings imported from England. It was the largest and grandest hotel of its day and the venue for glamorous weddings, Sunday curry tiffin lunches and tea dances. By the 1970's, however, the premises were overshadowed by bigger and more luxurious hotels. It was designated as a heritage monument and protected from demolition. However, in 1983 the Majestic closed and the National Art Gallery occupied the building for the next 15 years. Subsequently, the building was completely refurbished and has since been re-occupied by the Hotel Majestic, as a five-star establishment. The hotel forms a distinctive white landmark on raised ground and has rooftop garden views to Kuala Lumpur Station and across KL.

Sri Mahamariamman Temple, Chinatown

As I was driven back to the city centre there were hundreds of men leaving the mosque after Friday prayers. The taxi drove along a major highway as large crowds filed past the body of a dog that had been recently decapitated on the road. At KLCC I walked through the Suria shopping centre, which was particularly busy with people having just arrived from nearby mosques, many were wearing white Arabic *dishdashas*.

That evening I ate in a restaurant with a view across the KLCC park and lake, an oasis encircled by high-rise buildings. The lake featured dancing water fountains synchronised with a light show and musical accompaniment. It was watched by hundreds of people and was an impressive sight with the background of lit buildings.

West Coast Peninsular Malaysia

DAY 5
Kuala Lumpur to Ipoh

Kuala Lumpur Station

Kuala Lumpur *(Scheduled Departure 1304)* **to Ipoh** *(Scheduled Arrival 1520)* – ETS Gold

Ticket Cost: Ringgit 35 or US$9 in Economy Class Reserved Seats

The train to Ipoh arrived on time and was modern, clean and comfortable, almost full and thankfully air conditioned. Once we passed Putra Station we were into the outskirts of KL, and the high-rise buildings and Petronas Towers slipped away from view. This train moved at a fast pace and reached speeds of 150kph – it told me this on the TV screen in front. A woman nearby was having an argument on her smart phone. Later she left the carriage to continue her call and the intensity of the argument increased so that everyone could hear even more clearly: 'Stop calling my mother! I am not free. I don't want to see you.' Nearby passengers started to look about awkwardly. She returned sheepishly.

At Rawang Station the carriage filled up completely. Mr Bean and his clownish ways appeared on the TV, a staple diet of the traveling public in Asia, except on this train almost everyone was focused on their smart phones or sleeping. Forested hills began to appear in the background with some scarred and cleared patches of light brown. The foreground was mostly scrub vegetation with palm oil plantations in abundance and some plots of market gardening. Modern stations passed by with curved steel roofs and extra long platforms. We sped past large construction sites and drab towns and at Tanjong Malim crossed from Selangor State into Perak and then stopped at Slim River Station. This was the site of a major battle during WWII, which the British forces lost with heavy casualties, partly as a result of Japanese air superiority. It effectively ended Britain's hopes of defending Malaya. The Cameron Highlands drew closer and by the time we arrived at Kampar Station the forested mountains were in the near background with limestone outcrops visible.

A large cement plant came into view, then an attractive looking village with stilt houses and a large Chinese graveyard and lakes. Warehouses and modern housing

estates marked the emergence of Ipoh's outskirts. We arrived only a few minutes late at Ipoh, the terminus for the train. It has a grand whitewashed station that was built in 1917, and is referred to as the city's Taj Mahal, although there is a modern steel-roofed addition that extends over the platforms. AB Hubback, the same architect who designed Kuala Lumpur Station, provided the conceptual design, although this time there is less of a *mughal* theme and more features of late-Edwardian Baroque style. It originally incorporated a Majestic Hotel into the building, which has recently closed down. The main station building stands in a clear setting with no other structures to hinder views of it, unlike Kuala Lumpur Station.

New Town Ipoh

Outside there were many taxis, ramshackle ones of course, and a driver picked me out and we agreed a price to take me to

Kinta Limestone Hills

my hotel. As I approached the vehicle, I noticed there was someone else sitting in the passenger seat. 'Who's that?' I asked. 'A friend', said the driver. 'No', I said. The driver cursed. I wasn't about to take a chance with that situation and quickly found another taxi to take me. Soon after checking in I took a walk around the hotel's rundown area with its mix of Malay and Chinese restaurants. When I got back I went up to the hotel's rooftop bar to take in the twilight views over Ipoh's New Town with the dark shapes of the Cameron Highlands rising up in the distance.

Accommodation Suggestions (Ipoh):

Ibis Styles Hotel (www.accorhotels. com/gb/hotel-8650-ibis-styles-ipoh) - comfortable and modern three-star hotel located in the New Town area.

DAY 6
Ipoh to Taiping

Ipoh *(Scheduled Departure 1914)*
to Taiping *(Scheduled Arrival 2036)* –
Ekspres Rakyat

Ticket Cost: Ringgit 21 or US$5.5 in
AFC Premier Class Reserved Seats

Ipoh is named after a poisonous tree that used to be widespread in the area. Its location in the rich tin-bearing valley of the Kinta River led to rapid growth as a mining town, particularly during the 1920s and 1930s when it became one of the wealthiest cities in the world with the largest ownership of Mercedes Benz cars. Two of the main entertainment groups in Asia at the time, the Cathay Organisation and Shaw Brothers, set up cinemas in Ipoh. A Hakka miner, millionaire Yau Tet-Shin, began to develop a large area of the city in the early 1930s, now known as New Town, which extends eastwards from the Kinta River. In 1937, Ipoh was made the capital of Perak State, replacing Taiping, and is now one of the largest cities in the country with a population of 700,000.

The next morning was hot again as I sought out the coolest routes, primarily in the shade of arcaded buildings. I headed along Jalan Sultan Iskandar Shah towards the town centre. The frontage of this main road is comprised almost entirely of shop houses in varying condition. Just off one of the side streets are murals painted by street artists. There is also an old Rex Cinema building. I crossed the Kinta River and into Old Ipoh and walked towards the railway station passing people sketching buildings. Further on someone else was drawing and we started to talk. Casey was a retired architect based in Kuala Lumpur. He had lived in Ipoh when he was a young and moved to KL at 20. This was a trip down memory lane for him.

Jalan Sultan Iskandar Shop House, Ipoh

Once I got to Ipoh Station's expansive plaza area, dark clouds began to loom providing a dramatic setting for the two grand whitewashed neo-classical buildings, the railway station and Ipoh Town Hall. The

Town Hall, built in 1914, was also designed by AB Hubback, as was the adjoining Court House building. In the middle of this space is a memorial to those who lost their lives during the construction of the Thailand-Burma railway, as well as Perak residents who died in WWI and WWII.

It started to rain as I passed the mock-Tudor Royal Ipoh Club, and then back eastwards towards the Old Town alongside a large open space (the *padang*) where there were groups of people playing football ('AFC Grass Roots Football'). Part of the grass was marked out for a rugby pitch. Along one side are the grand colonial buildings of St. Michael's Institution, a large school founded by the Catholic La Sallean Brothers in 1927, later used by the Japanese as a regional headquarters (and torture chambers) after

Three-dimensional Street Art

they captured Ipoh in December 1941. Close by is the green and white Indian Muslim mosque built in 1908.

I was back near the Kinta River again and passed the former FMS (Federated Malay States) Bar and Restaurant, once the favoured retreat of colonial planters and miners for more than 100 years. From

Heritage Bank Building, Old Town Ipoh

there it was into the heart of Old Town, characterised by gridiron streets of shop houses. I came across a boutique café in a recently refurbished building for a decent coffee and cooling down, after which the owner showed me around the attractively restored premises. It was Sunday and the streets were quiet, although food courts and basic restaurants that I passed were full.

I followed the southern edge of the *padang* and its frontage of grand old bank buildings, testament to the town's earlier wealth. One is the former Mercantile Bank and dated 1931. This part of Ipoh is still occupied by most of Asia's best-known banks. It's also in this area that the well-known black and white former Perak Hydro building is located. The Perak Hydro-Electric Power Company was initially formed in London in 1926 to supply energy to the Kinta Valley tin mines and then moved in 1930 to its Ipoh building. It was the largest power supplier in Malaya at that time.

As I walked from Ipoh's 'banking quarter' I stumbled across an interestingly renovated part of Old Town. This is at the western end of the best-known part of Chinatown, Jalan Panglima, in the former Concubine Lane area. Jalan Panglima is Concubine Lane 3 of a series, which during the booming tin mining era was where tycoons would keep their mistresses and visit opium dens.

Many buildings along the alleyway were under renovation and included a mix of gift shops, cafes and basic restaurants. In a compact pedestrianised quarter there was a particularly popular area, which had been partly refurbished with some new building additions, all done with artsy touches. An English-style pub, Big Johns Music Shack, had been decorated in a 1960's/1970's UK retro style including posters of the Beatles and Liverpool's Cavern Club. Modern

Concubine Lane Renewal, Ipoh Old Town

restaurants were next to traditional Chinese cafes that had probably been there for some time. Old buildings mixed with new, trees had been retained and an intimate atmosphere formed part of a zany design setting. A band played in a small open space. The place was thriving and provided a stark contrast to the quiet surrounding streets. I had an enormous chicken *laksa* (Peranakan spicy noodle soup) in the minimalist styled Plan b restaurant. What was noticeable, as I wandered about, was the number of adverts for staff. Upgrading in Old Town Ipoh was experiencing problems with staff availability, and facing the fact that most locals headed to KL for higher wages.

I moved on through Chinatown's nostalgic charm and came across a group of people keeping puppies and kittens in pens 'for adoption'. A middle aged Chinese woman started to talk and offered to show me around Ipoh. Further southwards, across Jalan Iskandar Shah, the Old Town takes on a South Asian atmosphere with carpet and incense shops, Indian and Pakistani restaurants and food stores. Music boomed out from one of the buildings. The oldest temple in Ipoh, Paloh Ku Mia, built in 1872, is in this area close to the River Kinta.

Ipoh Town Hall

I took an eastwards direction through the busier commercial New Town area with its more recent shop houses. Near the hotel I passed an elderly Indian man sitting on the pavement who showed off his piercing whistle. When I walked past him he shouted 'Hey, Johnny! I'm an Indian superstar', and chuckled to himself. Soon after I got back to the hotel I was out and into a taxi by early evening.

The driver drove carefully through central Ipoh whilst listening to a Cantonese radio station. In the station waiting room a girl put her rucksack down nearby and wandered off. Very trusting, I thought! Later, we began to chat. Omori was on a 'traveling adventure', she told me, at the end of which she would return to Japan to help her parents run a guest house at the foot of Mount Fuji. Her trip started in Mongolia, then Singapore and she was now on her way to Bangkok. She spoke fluent English and appeared to be adventurous and independent.

As the train pulled out of Ipoh Station the sun began to set. We made one stop at Kuala Kangsar before arriving at Taiping Station. I waved goodbye to Omori as she was in the middle of chatting to someone else. Taxis were difficult to find at the station so I asked a railway official in broken Malay if he could call for one. Not long afterwards it arrived to take me through darkened streets to my centrally-located hotel on Taiping's main street, Jalan Kota.

Accommodation Suggestions (Taiping):

Hotel Panorama (www.panoramataiping. com) - basic but reasonably comfortable city centre hotel.

Villa Sentosa (www.sentosa-villa.com) - a rustic alternative on the eastern edge of Taiping near Bukit Larut.

West Coast Peninsular Malaysia

DAY 7
Taiping

Taiping is the oldest and second largest town in Perak State. It experiences more rain than any other urban area in Peninsular Malaysia and this has contributed to a variety of flora and century-old rain trees in the Taiping Lake Gardens, established in 1884 in an abandoned tin mine. Nearby Bukit Larut (formerly Maxwell Hill) is the first hill station in Malaysia with existing colonial bungalows built in 1879. Taiping developed quickly in the mid-19th Century after the discovery of tin, as the mines attracted large numbers of Chinese settlers.

Fighting between different groups of migrant secret societies, principally between the Hakka and Cantonese, became so disruptive that in the early 1870s the British intervened and took control. The town was once known as Klian ('mine') Pauh ('mango') but was renamed Taiping ('everlasting peace') in 1874 to commemorate the end of the Larut War fought between mining groups.

I left the hotel to search for breakfast in a nearby newly built shopping mall. After a baked cheese fish meal, served up by a tiny bird-like waitress in a *hijab* who was sweet and smiley, I walked the short distance to a tourist information centre in the clock tower building, where helpful staff advised

Former Hotel Peace, Taiping

St. George's School, Taiping

on what to see. The building was a former fire station, built in 1890, and marks the centre of town. Walking westwards along Jalan Kota I came across the traditional old wooden market. Southwards from there, on the corner of Jalan Panggung Wayang, is a beautiful terrace of ornately decorated shop houses once occupied by the Hotel Peace. The old hotel sign is still there. Northwards along Jalan Masjid is the Old Kota Mosque, built in 1897.

There are two former colonial schools on Jalan Stesen, St. George's School (1915) and King Edward VII School (1905), which are the grandest buildings in Taiping. Just a little further along this street is a beautifully ornate building, probably used as a Chinese ancestral home or clan house. On either side of the elaborate wooden door are inscriptions that, roughly translated, state: 'The ancestral family's prestige and reputation is like a flowing river'; and, 'Families experience hardships in their journeys to come to this beautiful country to live, work and rest here'.

Opposite is the old railway station, now occupied by offices, that was the terminus for the first railway line in Malaysia, built in 1885. With the town's mining industry thriving, this 14km line transported tin to Port Weld (now known as Kuala Sepetang), as well as mine workers to their settlements. Railway connections were expanded in the 1930s to Ipoh, KL and Singapore, but in the 1980s the Port Weld line was dismantled.

Jalan Stesen Shop House Entrance

Jalan Stesen Shop House Window

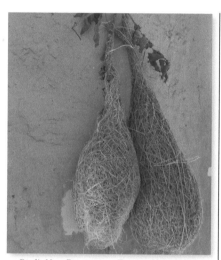

Bird's Nest Decoration, Taiping Shop House

Padang Building

Across from the King Edward VII School and its splendid grounds is the Old Rest House, which is now derelict. I explored its eerie and overgrown buildings, and

a small abandoned pool in its central courtyard, trying to imagine better times. Nearby is the whitewashed neo-colonial building of the District Office and adjoining it the *padang* with a bandstand placed at the base of a forested hill. This rectangular space is enclosed by stilted former mansions, probably once occupied by colonial government officials, but now used principally as military offices. At one corner is the wooden All Saints Church (1886), as well as a cemetery full of colonial graves. One poignant gravestone marks the resting place of brothers Simeon and Arthur Kennedy who died in the 1920s at the ages of ten and twelve respectively.

At the northeastern corner of the *padang* is the New Club, built in 1885, that still has the original wooden whitewashed

All Saints Church

Taiping Lake Gardens

and stilted building. From here there is an attractive view of the greenery of Taiping Lake Gardens (*Taman Tasik Taiping*) stretching out below, with trees and lakes, and a backdrop of Bukit Larut to the east. The park is notable for the many rain trees, mostly fringing the lake gardens, which are more than a century old. Taiping Zoo is on the park's eastern side.

I followed the lakeside edges: Swan Lake; Jungle Lake; and, South Lake, and crossed promontories and over bridges, past bamboo groves and groups of large exotic trees set around the still water. At the uninspiring Flemington Hotel there are views from its rooftop across the landscape of gardens and lakes. Taiping's heritage buildings are more spread out and less intact than in Ipoh. However, the lakeside gardens were a very definite plus point for the town. I returned to my hotel after a short and sharp rainstorm, which provided much relief from the sweltering conditions earlier. The aftermath resulted in an atmospheric scene of mist rolling down from the surrounding mountains.

DAY 8
Taiping to Alor Star (and Langkawi)

Taiping *(Scheduled Departure 0330)* **to Alor Star** *(Scheduled Arrival 0756)* – Ekspres Rakyat

Ticket Cost: Ringgit 21 or US$5.5 in AFC Superior Class Reserved Seats

Another disheveled taxi took me from the hotel in the very early morning. The driver drew nonchalantly on his cigarette, as he made his way through the town's dark and empty streets to the station. The train from KL had carriages of mostly bunk sleeper beds but I settled into a reserved seat in the reclining 'Superior' class, which was almost full. Behind me was a lively group of

Indians chattering away with the carriage lights providing almost daylight brightness. This last leg of the railway journey would be tiring and uncomfortable and there would be little sleep. There were also some suspicious groups of Malay boys (in twos and threes) wandering up and down the aisles, standing around the toilet areas and peering a little too inquisitively into the carriages.

We stopped at a number of small towns, again with large modern stations before arriving at Bukit Mertajam. The train then pulled out onto a spur line to Butterworth Station where there were ferries to Penang Island and Georgetown. I looked out at Butterworth's grim industrial facilities, brightly lit refineries and chemical plants, factories and warehouses. Most passengers got off at Butterworth and the rest waited for about twenty minutes for the train to

Alor Star Area Landscape

Kuala Kedah Fishing Boats

fill up again before continuing. The engine passed by to hitch on to the carriages and take us back to Bukit Mertajam at a crawl. As we left Bukit Mertajam for a second time, the sky started to glow in a pinkish red with a sunrise creeping above the palm oil plantations. This light reflected off the rivers that we crossed. A market next to Sungai Petani Station got into the trading swing. We passed estates of cheaply built bungalows and of course more palm oil plantations. After Gurun the train crossed a flat landscape of rice paddies that stretched into the distance with low hills in the far background and mist rising up. The hills disappeared as we approached Alor Star and followed the North-South Expressway heading towards Thailand.

I got off the train at Alor Star, the capital of Kedah State. It wasn't long before I was being driven in another scruffy taxi to Kuala Kedah, the port for Langkawi Island. Alor Star is considered to be a predominantly conservative Malay city, although there are a number of Thai temples as well as a small Chinatown. It's the birthplace of the former prime minister of Malaysia, Dr. Mahathir

Mohamad. At first glance it looked to be a pleasant and well-kept town with attractive terraced shop houses and parks. We arrived 15 minutes later at Kuala Kedah with its interesting looking fort, built in 1770, opposite the fishing port. Ferries to Langkawi run on a regular basis, although this was low season. The next ferry would be at 9.30am, with a journey of an hour and forty-five minutes, and a good time for me to catch up on sleep.

Berjaya Langkawi Resort Mountain Backdrop

Kuala Kedah to Langkawi Ferry

Langkawi is the main coastal resort destination in Malaysia, and more popular than Pulau Tioman on the east coast or Batu Ferringhi on Penang Island. During this trip headline news was reporting on thousands of Bangladeshi and Rohingya migrants landing by boat in western Malaysia. A few hundred had arrived in Langkawi.

The island's main port (Kuah Town), which was in the process of being upgraded, had the distinct atmosphere of a tourist area. Cafes and gift shops occupied the port's arrival area. Soon, a cheery taxi driver took me through the compact Kuah Town towards the western side of the island. Langkawi is forested and mountainous and has three UNESCO World GeoPark sites. One of these is Mount Mat Chincang, thought to be the oldest geological formation in Malaysia and next to the Berjaya Langkawi Resort. Consequently, the resort is set in an extremely attractive landscape with a beautiful coastline and a stunning green

Berjaya Langkawi Resort Forest Villas

and rugged mountainous backdrop. The wooden stilted villas are lined along the coastline, either as water bungalows or set into the steep forested hills. There was a strong feeling of being amongst nature and wildlife with the background noise of chattering monkeys. It was as stark a contrast as there could be with the beginning of the journey from Singapore Woodlands.

Accommodation Suggestions (Langkawi):

Berjaya Langkawi Resort (www.berjayahotel.com/langkawi) comfortable five-star resort hotel set in beautiful natural surroundings.

SOUTH EAST ASIAN RAILWAY JOURNEYS:

1 **Bangkok to Singapore**
2 **Bangkok to Chiang Mai**
3 **Bangkok to Vientiane**
4 **Jakarta to Malang (South Java)**
5 **Hanoi to Saigon**
6 **Jakarta to Banyuwangi (and Bali)**
7 **Through Malaysia**